USING THE POWER WITHIN

Pastor George Allen Blacken, Sr.

Apostolic Pentecostal Alliance Books LLC

WALDORF, MARYLAND

Copyright © 2018 by George Allen Blacken
All rights reserved.

No part of this book may be used or reproduced in any manner without written permission of the author, except for brief quotations used in reviews and critiques.

Printed in the United States of America

Published by Apostolic Pentecostal Alliance Books LLC, Maryland
www.apabooksllc.com

The Apostolic Pentecostal Alliance Books LLC name, logo, and colophon are the trademarks of Apostolic Pentecostal Alliance Books LLC.

ISBN: 978-0-9989630-2-0 (Printed Edition)
ISBN: 978-0-9989630-3-7 (E-Book Edition)

First Edition 2018

Write inquiries to:

Apostolic Pentecostal Alliance Books LLC
150 Post Office Road
P.O. Box 1813
Waldorf, MD 20601

Table of Contents

Chapter 1: The Triune Man……..………..4

Chapter 2: How Mankind Lost the Power………………..………………………10

Chapter 3: You Can Have the Power…...19

Chapter 4: Boundaries of Power…....…..26

Chapter 5: Using the Power Within for Your Life…………………..……………..41

Chapter 1: The Triune Man

A realm is a domain where things happen. There are three primary domains where we as human beings, interface with: 1) Spiritual Realm, 2) Mental Realm, and 3) Physical Realm. The Spiritual Realm is normally not detected by the human senses, but yet has the greatest influence on the other realms. Our physical senses are designed to perceive material things, not people, things, and locations which are immaterial.

> *While we look not at the things which are seen, but at the things which are not seen: for the things which are seen are temporal; but the things which are not seen are eternal.*
>
> - *II Corinthians 4:18*

There are barriers limiting communication and other interactions between the three realms, especially between the Spiritual and Physical realms. There are also still limitations between the Mental and Physical realms with the average human being not being able to regularly perform, telepathy, telekinesis, pyrokinesis, or other material and environmental transformations with just thoughts. We can discern, perceive, or observe, but are not mind readers.

The Spiritual Realm consists of spiritual beings and locations such as God and His angels which reside in Heaven, Satan and his demonic forces, those we have declared as physically dead (both good and evil), Hell, Lake of Fire, and every supernatural force and mystical influence in existence which is derived from either God or Satan. The Mental Realm pertains to our minds, dreams, and the psychological elements influenced by the other realms. The Physical Realm consists of the material things, people, and locations we can communicate and interact with through our physical senses.

Before we go any further, it must be made clear that the Spiritual Realm is no hoax. The undeniable source of proof for the invisible things in the Spiritual Realm are the visible things in the Physical Realm.

> *For the invisible things of Him from the creation of the world are clearly seen, being understood by the things that are made, even His eternal power and Godhead; so that they are without excuse*
>
> - *Romans 1:20*
>
> *Through faith we understand that the worlds were framed by the word of God, so that things which are seen were not made of things which do appear.*
>
> - *Hebrews 11:3*

In spite of what we experience through our physical senses, nothing randomly happens in the Physical Realm. Everything that occurs in the Physical Realm is influenced by the Spiritual Realm. God can create something out of nothing that will appear in the Physical Realm through just the words He speaks from the Spiritual Realm. With just our physical and mental resources, we can only create something new by modifying material that already exists. We can either help preserve life or take life, but cannot create life. Even childbirth requires a supernatural encounter to bring that which is naturally conceived to life. It takes God to breath in you and make you a living soul.

> *And the Lord God formed man of the dust of the ground, and breathed into his nostrils the breath of life; and man became a living soul.*
>
> - *Genesis 2:7*

You are made in the image of God consisting of three components: 1) Body, 2) Soul, and 3) Spirit.

> *And the very God of peace sanctify you wholly; and I pray God your whole spirit and soul and body be preserved blameless unto the coming of our Lord Jesus Christ.*
>
> - *I Thessalonians 5:23*

Most realize the body is the physical, material component which decays and eventually dies. Until the time that you leave this earth, your body serves as a temple in which your soul and spirit dwell in. You use your body to interact with the physical realm. Because of your body, you, through your physical senses of hearing, sight, smell, touch, taste, and equilibrium have world consciousness. Feeling is the voice of the body. Both the spirit and soul are non-material, but there is a difference between the two. The soul is not your life force, but includes your imagination, memories, reasoning, and affections. Your soul is your mind. The soul links your body and spirit. Your soul gives you self-consciousness. Reason is the voice of the soul or mind. From Genesis 2:7, we see that it takes God to give a soul life. A life force needs to be placed in the soul. The spirit is your life force. Your spirit is who you are (also your heart) and makes you capable of God-consciousness and communication with God. Your spirit is your link to the Spiritual Realm. Conscience is the voice of the spirit. Your will is also part of your heart. You are a spirit with a soul in a body.

Chapter 2: How Mankind Lost the Power

Power is the authority or ability to make decisions or change the outcome of a situation. Authority is delegated power. It makes things happen. Ability is the right combination of understanding and skill to accomplish what you desire to do. God made Adam and Eve the most powerful beings on Earth, giving them full authority over the Earth. They also had the necessary abilities to retain control over the Earth with there not being the present barriers between the Spiritual, Mental, and Physical realms. God talks with them as people physically talk with and hear from each other.

So God created man in his own image, in the image of God created he him; male and female created he them. And God blessed them, and God said unto them, Be fruitful, and multiply, and replenish the earth, and subdue it: and have dominion over the fish of the sea, and over the fowl of the air, and over every living thing that moveth upon the earth. And God said, Behold, I have given you every herb bearing seed, which is upon the face of all the earth, and every tree, in the which is the fruit of a tree yielding seed; to you it shall be for meat. And to every beast of the earth, and to every fowl of the air, and to everything that creepeth upon the earth, wherein there is life, I have given every green herb for meat: and it was so.

- *Genesis 1:27-30*

In this perfect scenario, Adam and Eve only had one commandment, which was to not eat any fruit from the Tree of Knowledge of Good and Evil, or else the consequence would be death as commanded by God Himself in Genesis 2:16-17. God owned the Earth and made Adam the landlord, but there was an intruder on the Earth, who would eventually make his presence known, Satan. When reading Genesis 1:6-8, it can be noticed that the second day of Earth's creation is the only day of creation that the Lord did call good. During this second day of creation the sky was separated from the sea because previously the whole Earth was filled with frozen water like something you would picture from an ice age. As described in Ephesians 2:2, Satan is *the prince of the power of the air, the spirit that now worketh in the children of disobedience*. The Lord noticed Satan's intrusion on the Earth when the second day of creation was completed.

Unfortunately, Adam and Eve disobeyed God and this led to multiple consequences in all three realms. Focusing on the power that was lost, such consequences included:

1. Losing power over evil. As shown when God confronted Adam and Eve in Genesis chapter 3, they picked up a new sinful nature not desiring the presence of God and accountability to His authority. As a result, we were all born as sinners with a nature wanting to disobey God.

For all have sinned, and come short of the glory of God

- *Romans 3:23*

2. Losing power over death. Adam sinned against God and all of mankind was given a double death sentence as a result, evidenced by physical death mankind experiences (sickness and decay are bi-products coming from the sin resulting in the pronounced

death sentence) and eternal death, which God came in the form of Jesus to save us from.

> *For the wages of sin is death; but the gift of God is eternal life through Jesus Christ our Lord.*
>
> - *Romans 6:23*

3. Losing power over Earth. Creation itself changed when Adam sinned. Adam no longer had dominion over the Earth. The animal and plant kingdoms no longer instantly obeyed Adam and Eve, catering to their every need and whim. All Adam previously had to do was speak a word, but must now work for everything. Mankind and animal would overall form more of an adversarial relationship between each other and many men and women would conflict with each other more than complement each other as God intended. Instead of man being one with the Earth, he lost his place in the world trying to once again subdue it

through material means rather than the supernatural power previously given to him by God. Man would compete for resources more than sharing with each other, leading to continual poverty, violence, and other vices among the population. Further complicating matters, when Adam sinned against God, thus rejecting God's authority, Adam gave authority of the Earth over to the devil. The devil went from intruder to landlord of the Earth as evidenced by the devil tempting Jesus with the kingdoms of the Earth if He would bow down to him during Jesus' temptation in the wilderness.

> *Again, the devil taketh Him up into an exceeding high mountain, and sheweth Him all the kingdoms of the world, and the glory of them; And saith unto Him, All these things will I give thee, if thou wilt fall down and worship me. Then saith Jesus unto him, Get thee hence, Satan: for it is written, Thou shalt worship the Lord thy God, and Him only shalt thou serve.*

- *Matthew 4:8-10*

Whatever lease Adam had on this Earth will determine how long it will take for Satan's presence to be completely removed from the Earth. When this lease expires, the time will come for Satan's presence to be completely removed from the Earth. Satan's demonic forces realize this.

> *And when He was come to the other side into the country of the Gergesenes, there met Him two possessed with devils, coming out of the tombs, exceeding fierce, so that no man might pass by that way. And, behold, they cried out, saying, What have we to do with thee, Jesus, thou Son of God? art thou come hither to torment us before the time? And there was a good way off from them an herd of many swine feeding. So the devils besought Him, saying, If thou cast us out, suffer us to go away into the herd of swine. And He said unto them, Go. And when they were come out, they went into the herd of swine: and, behold, the whole herd of*

swine ran violently down a steep place into the sea, and perished in the waters. And they that kept them fled, and went their ways into the city, and told everything, and what was befallen to the possessed of the devils.

- *Matthew 8:28-33*

4. Losing power over evil spiritual forces. Adam's sin also resulted in mankind being handicapped with there now being barriers placed between the Spiritual, Mental, and Physical realms that were previously not present. Adam lost connection with God and as a result, we are all naturally born with our spirit being in a dormant state, dead to the things of God, lacking the connection to the Spiritual Realm.

But the natural man receiveth not the things of the Spirit of God: for they are foolishness unto him: neither can he know them, because they are spiritually discerned.

- *I Corinthians 2:14*

Even with our spirit in a dormant state, God still speaks to our conscience, but only a few accept His invitation.

> *For many are called, but few are chosen.*

- *Matthew 22:14*

Without that spiritual connection with the Lord, we do not have the spiritual power needed to overcome the power of Satan and his demonic forces who work from the Spiritual Realm.

Chapter 3: You Can Have the Power

All is not lost. God came in the form of Jesus Christ to destroy the works of the devil in our lives.

> *He that committeth sin is of the devil; for the devil sinneth from the beginning. For this purpose the Son of God was manifested, that he might destroy the works of the devil.*
>
> - *I John 3:8*
>
> *For God so loved the world, that he gave his only begotten Son, that whosoever believeth in him should not perish, but have everlasting life.*
>
> - *John 3:16*

At the cross, Jesus died for the sin of mankind, which started with Adam. No one else could serve as the perfect, unblemished sacrifice acceptable to God other than Jesus. When Jesus paid the price of sin for mankind, He did experience death. Jesus' work at the cross did not stop there or else it would all be for nothing. I Corinthians 15:17 reminds us, *if Christ be not raised, your faith is vain; ye are yet in your sins.*

Satan's authority over the Earth and the grip of death were so great that when the Old Testament saints died, they could not go to where God resides in heaven.

> *The sting of death is sin; and the strength of sin is the law.*
>
> - *I Corinthians 15:56*

No one can carry sin with them to heaven. Animal sacrifices only deferred judgment, but did not get rid of sin. The Old Testament saints' faith in the true living God was so strong that even though they did descend into the underworld when they died, they were placed in a separate paradise compartment of the underworld by God. The parable of the rich man and Lazarus taught by Jesus from Luke 16:19-31 revealed to us that during those times, there were two areas of the underworld, Paradise and Hell separated by a great gulf that no one can cross. When Jesus died, He ascended into the underworld and Satan and all of his demonic forces tried to keep Jesus down. Despite Satan's best attempts, his forces were confused and defeated by Jesus Christ after the third day.

> *And having spoiled principalities and powers, He made a shew of them openly, triumphing over them in it.*
>
> - *Colossians 2:15*

At this moment, death was defeated and Satan was dethroned. Jesus reclaimed everything Adam lost and Satan was demoted from landlord to an unwelcomed tenant of the Earth, no longer having authority over it. The resurrected Jesus ascended into heaven to present His blood sacrifice to the heavenly altar making what He accomplished through the cross and His resurrection effectual for all believers throughout all time. According to Ephesians 1:20, Jesus is now seated at the right hand of God with right hand representing highest authority. The resurrected Jesus reminded His disciples in Matthew 28:18, *All power is given unto me in Heaven and in Earth.* Jesus Christ did not ascend alone.

> *And the graves were opened; and many bodies of the saints which slept arose, And came out of the graves after his resurrection, and went into the holy city, and appeared unto many.*
>
> - *Matthew 27:52-53*

When Jesus left the underworld and arose, the Old Testament saints also arose and ascended.

Having the right hand of authority, Jesus Christ is the head over all things to the true Church. It is for our sake that He's the head, so that we through Him might exercise that authority over all things.

> *And hath put all things under his feet, and gave him to be the head over all things to the church, Which is his body, the fulness of him that filleth all in all.*
>
> - *Ephesians 1:22-23*

The Head (Jesus) and the Body (Church) are one. We were raised up together. The authority was conferred upon the Head and the Body. You have the spiritual power right now in this life!

> *Even when we were dead in sins, hath quickened us together with Christ, (by grace ye are saved;) And hath raised us up together, and made us sit together in heavenly places in Christ Jesus*

- *Ephesians 2:5-6*

When someone becomes a born again, spirit filled believer, his or her spiritual standing is raised to heavenly places with Jesus Christ. This standing gives us authority, power from God Himself. We, the Church, are part of the Kingdom of God; Satan has no right to rule us or dominate us. Born again believers who continue to live spirit filled lives are no longer the authority of the forces of darkness. Satan and his forces and those he influences no longer have the power to stop our purpose or deny us our true destiny. We actually have power over demonic forces.

> *Giving thanks unto the Father, which hath made us meet to be partakers of the inheritance of the saints in light: Who hath delivered us from the power of darkness, and hath translated us into the kingdom of His dear Son*
>
> - *Colossians 1:12-13*

Jesus already defeated and dethroned Satan at His resurrection. When Jesus physically returns to Earth, He will send one of His angels to swiftly evict Satan from the Earth. Jesus has already given us the victory and the power to enforce such. It is our responsibility to believe, receive, and enforce what the Lord has given us. You can have the power. Do not deny what belongs to you.

Chapter 4: Boundaries of Power

What supernatural power did our creator, God Himself, make available for us? How can we utilize this power to change our lives? First, the principles of power must be understood.

> *But he that knew not, and did commit things worthy of stripes, shall be beaten with few stripes. For unto whomsoever much is given, of him shall be much required: and to whom men have committed much, of him they will ask the more.*
>
> - *Luke 12:48*

What is required of us? This is best understood through realizing that in fictional material, supernatural powers and laws are constrained only be an author's imagination, but in reality, the supernatural comes exclusively from the Spiritual Realm, God or the devil. Whoever you bow down to will determine the power, influence, and destiny that you will have. Your weakest, least successful people on this Earth are those who have not bowed down to either. Your more powerful, influential, and wealthiest people in the world are those who have bowed to God or the devil. Supernatural power comes from God or the devil. Never forget that the invisible things drive the visible things. Who you bow down to will be your source of power and John 15:18-20 communicates whoever hears your benefactor will hear you as well. The temptation that Jesus faced in the wilderness is the same temptation that every individual who desires to achieve new thresholds of success and influence and miraculous prosperity in their lives.

> *Again, the devil taketh Him up into an exceeding high mountain, and sheweth Him all the kingdoms of the world, and the glory of them; And saith unto Him, All these things will I give thee, if thou wilt fall down and worship me. Then saith Jesus unto him, Get thee hence, Satan: for it is written, Thou shalt worship the Lord thy God, and Him only shalt thou serve.*
>
> - *Matthew 4:8-10*

Choose carefully, because there is a price to pay having eternal consequences.

> *For what shall it profit a man, if he shall gain the whole world, and lose his own soul? Or what shall a man give in exchange for his soul?*
>
> - *Mark 8:36-37*

Matthew 6:21 and Luke 12:34 remind us, *For where your treasure is, there will your heart be also.* Satan will tempt you to bow down to him based on what or who you treasure most. Who you bow down to is who you submit to. That is who you agree with and obey. It is sad that many people have bowed down to Satan to achieve their political, economic, or social desires. The growing memberships in secret societies, cults, and gatherings involving witchcraft can be alarming, but all involved with such are on the losing side. Jesus already defeated Satan. The power (Jesus) that backs your authority is greater than that which backs those who have bowed down to Satan.

> *Ye are of God, little children, and have overcome them: because greater is He that is in you, than he that is in the world.*
>
> - *I John 4:4*

Now that you know the sources of supernatural power, such power only manifests itself in the Physical Realm from the Spiritual Realm to perform the will of your benefactor. You are the vessel, not the controller. When God's will is not in something, the power will not manifest. With demonic power, Satan will give you the illusion of control, when you are really his puppet. One other note with this is that even when the power of God is backing you, you are not authorized to be arrogant, foolish, or purposely put yourself in dangerous, questionable situations. We strongly encourage you to not tempt God and not take His Word out of context!

> *Then the devil taketh him up into the holy city, and setteth him on a pinnacle of the temple, And saith unto him, If thou be the Son of God, cast thyself down: for it is written, He shall give his angels charge concerning thee: and in their hands they shall bear thee up, lest at any time thou dash thy foot against a stone. Jesus said unto him, It is written again, Thou shalt not tempt the Lord thy God.*
>
> *-   Matthew 4:5-7*

The power from God gives you greater control over yourself while the demonic power takes control of you. The power from God prompts you, but the demonic power possesses you. The power from God saves, delivers you. The demonic power condemns, inevitably destroys you. The power from God gives you continual prosperity, but demonic power only gives an illusion of prosperity for a season. The latter also brings curses instead of blessings to your loved ones.

> *Be not deceived; God is not mocked: for whatsoever a man soweth, that shall he also reap. For he that soweth to his flesh shall of the flesh reap corruption; but he that soweth to the Spirit shall of the Spirit reap life everlasting.*
>
> - *Galatians 6:7-8*

Getting back to the power from God prompting you, what prompts you? Remember, that conscience is the voice of the spirit. God speaks to our hearts.

> *The spirit of man is the candle of the Lord, searching all the inward parts of the belly.*
>
> - *Proverbs 20:27*

From natural birth, our spirit is initially in a dormant state, only occasionally hearing from God through the conscience in our hearts. We need something to reawaken our spirit and resurrect our spiritual connection with God if we are going to be able to utilize the power He has made available to us. In addition to having our sins forgiven, this is the purpose of spiritual rebirth. Some examples of spiritual rebirth are provided in Acts 2:37-39, Acts 8:5-24, Acts 10:44-48, and Acts 19:1-6. When further examining Acts 2:1-11 and the previous examples from chapters 8, 10, and 19 of the book of Acts in the bible, evidence is provided for knowing if you have the power inside of you. You do not have the power within if you are not filled with God's Holy Spirit. The evidence of the invisible things are shown through the visible things. God did provide us with such visible evidence of having the power within us through us spontaneously speaking in a language we are not trained to speak through God prompting us to do such through His Holy Spirit. Speaking in tongues is the visible supernatural sign that the power of God is in us. When God speaks to us, John 15:26 reminds us His spirit will only testify of Him, His Word.

> *And when the day of Pentecost was fully come, they were all with one accord in one place. And suddenly there came a sound from heaven as of a rushing mighty wind, and it filled all the house where they were sitting. And there appeared unto them cloven tongues like as of fire, and it sat upon each of them. And they were all filled with the Holy Ghost, and began to speak with other tongues, as the Spirit gave them utter-*

ance. And there were dwelling at Jerusalem Jews, devout men, out of every nation under heaven. Now when this was noised abroad, the multitude came together, and were confounded, because that every man heard them speak in his own language. And they were all amazed and marvelled, saying one to another, Behold, are not all these which speak Galilaeans? And how hear we every man in our own tongue, wherein we were born? Parthians, and Medes, and Elamites, and the dwellers in Mesopotamia, and in Judaea, and Cappadocia, in Pontus, and Asia, Phrygia, and Pamphylia, in Egypt, and in the parts of Libya about Cyrene, and strangers of Rome, Jews and proselytes, Cretes and Arabians, we do hear them speak in our tongues the wonderful works of God.

- *Acts 2:1-11*

The power did not become inaccessible to us when the early church died. This promise is made available to all generations because what Jesus accomplished on the cross and His resurrection is good for all in this church period who believe and receive the promises of God.

> *For the promise is unto you, and to your children, and to all that are afar off, even as many as the Lord our God shall call.*
>
> - *Acts 2:39*

Power and purpose are married to one another. You are given power to accomplish God's will for a specific purpose. Vision is understanding God's purpose for you. The Holy Spirit will anoint you for God's intended purpose for you. Anointing is the God given ability to accomplish something that is the Lord's will for you to do. The effectiveness and portion of your anointing are tied to your purpose and commitment to God's will. The manifestations of the power of the Holy Spirit are dependent upon both the emergent need and the purpose given to you by God. A manifestation is visible evidence in the Physical Realm that something supernatural from the Spiritual Realm has occurred.

> *But all these worketh that one and the selfsame Spirit, dividing to every man severally as He will.*
>
> - *I Corinthians 12:11*

Something else to remember concerning manifestations of the power of the Holy Spirit, is that we can experience a spiritual overflow through fervent prayers, committed meditation on God's Word, and spirit filled praise and worship. When we experience a spiritual overflow, the power of God's Holy Spirit shall manifest.

> *Wherefore be ye not unwise, but understanding what the will of the Lord is. And be not drunk with wine, wherein is excess; but be filled with the Spirit; Speaking to yourselves in psalms and hymns and spiritual songs, singing and making melody in your heart to the Lord; Giving thanks always for all things unto God and the Father in the name of our Lord Jesus Christ; Submitting yourselves one to another in the fear of God.*
>
> - *Ephesians 5:17-21*

This is one of the reasons why the devil has infiltrated praise and worship in many church services so that the power will not be manifested to minister to people in the audience.

When you are filled with the Holy Spirit, your words literally carry power.

> *For verily I say unto you, That whosoever shall say unto this mountain, Be thou removed, and be thou cast into the sea; and shall not doubt in his heart, but shall believe that those things which he saith shall come to pass; he shall have whatsoever he saith. Therefore I say unto you, What things soever ye desire, when ye pray, believe that ye receive them, and ye shall have them.*

- *Mark 11:23-24*

Believing is trusting and obeying God's Word, receiving is counting God's promise as already done, even if there is no physical evidence of anything changing, confessing is acknowledging and speaking God's Word or will into your life or another's situation, and enforcing is using spiritual authority to uphold the victory the Lord has already given you. The authority behind your words come from speaking in the name of Jesus and only saying those things that are

God's will. You have a covenant with God through Jesus Christ and this covenant results in you being adopted as a child of God. You make a demand in the name of Jesus and you make a request to your heavenly Father, God, in the name of Jesus.

> *Verily, verily, I say unto you, He that believeth on me, the works that I do shall he do also; and greater works than these shall he do; because I go unto my Father. And whatsoever ye shall ask in my name, that will I do, that the Father may be glorified in the Son. If ye shall ask any thing in my name, I will do it.*
>
> - *John 14:12-14*

James 4:7 reminds us, *Submit yourselves therefore to God. Resist the devil, and he will flee from you.* We have authority to overcome or bind demonic forces, but we do not have control over another human being's free will. Once the Lord has given you the authority and anointing, you must do for yourself through the power of the Lord's might. Do not ask for something you already have. The Lord will not bail you out if He has already given you the solution, the power.

Chapter 5: Using the Power Within for Your Life

Many times, before our situations change, we must change ourselves. It is through the power of the Holy Spirit dwelling on the inside, we can live a lifestyle overcoming the sinful nature and temptations that once dominated us. You now have full power over yourself.

> *For if ye live after the flesh, ye shall die: but if ye through the Spirit do mortify the deeds of the body, ye shall live. For as many as are led by the Spirit of God, they are the sons of God.*
>
> - *Romans 8:13-14*

The power of loosing and binding belong to you. You have the power to loose blessings into your life and loose people free from demonic possession or persuasion. You have the power to bind demonic forces and their influences on your life and your interactions with other people.

> *Verily I say unto you, Whatsoever ye shall bind on earth shall be bound in heaven: and whatsoever ye shall loose on earth shall be loosed in heaven.*
>
> - *Matthew 18:18*
>
> *Submit yourselves therefore to God. Resist the devil, and he will flee from you.*
>
> - *James 4:7*

After a demonic influence has been removed from a person and they choose to still remain an obstacle, you have the authority to ask the Lord to remove such an individual from your life or place of influence in your life in the name of Jesus. You are not physically trying to or mentally wishing someone's death or demise. You are turning to the Lord to remove the obstacle, whichever way He chooses. The Lord may even convict and change someone's heart.

> *For verily I say unto you, That whosoever shall say unto this mountain, Be thou removed, and be thou cast into the sea; and shall not doubt in his heart, but shall believe that those things which he saith shall come to pass; he shall have whatsoever he saith.*
>
> - *Mark 11:23*

A mountain is any obstacle, whether it be people, debt, or anything else standing in the way of your purpose and progress. You have the power to speak and demand whatever the mountain is to be removed in the name of Jesus! If you believe, receive, and confess, the obstacle shall be removed at God's appointed time! Make sure you remain in the perfect will of God, grow, and fulfill whatever objectives He intended to be accomplished through your experience.

Being a born again believer, filled with the Holy Spirit, you are no longer under the Curse of the Law, as described in Deuteronomy 28:15-68, which is sickness, poverty, and eternal death. You have both the favor and authority to remove sickness and poverty from your life. You have the authority to rebuke the demonic forces' dealings in these matters and access God's promised blessings to supply for your needs and open doors for you that no man or woman can shut.

> *Christ hath redeemed us from the curse of the law, being made a curse for us: for it is written, Cursed is every one that hangeth on a tree*
>
> *- Galatians 3:13*
>
> *And these signs shall follow them that believe; In my name shall they cast out devils; they shall speak with new tongues; they shall take up serpents; and*

if they drink any deadly thing, it shall not hurt them; they shall lay hands on the sick, and they shall recover.

- Mark 16:17-18

Beloved, I wish above all things that thou mayest prosper and be in health, even as thy soul prospereth.

- III John 1:2

I know thy works: behold, I have set before thee an open door, and no man can shut it: for thou hast a little strength, and hast kept my word, and hast not denied my name.

- Revelation 3:8

As Romans 8:31 emphasized, *What shall we then say to these things? If God be for us, who can be against us?* If God is for you completing your purpose and you are dedicated to fulfilling such, no person, sickness, or other factor can stop or take you out before it is finished.

> *Being confident of this very thing, that He which hath begun a good work in you will perform it until the day of Jesus Christ*
>
> - *Philippians 1:6*
>
> *And the Lord shall deliver me from every evil work, and will preserve me unto His heavenly kingdom: to whom be glory for ever and ever. Amen.*
>
> - *II Timothy 4:18*

To support purpose, deliverance, and spiritual maturity, the Lord has given the church the gifts (I Corinthians 12:8-10), administrations (Ephesians 4:8-16 and I Corinthians 12:28-30), and operations (Mark 16:17-18, Acts 5:1-10, and Acts 13:6-12) of the Holy Spirit. He has given all spirit filled believers power! Seek and ye shall find. God is no respecter of persons.

Finally, always remember from Psalm 119:89, *Forever, O Lord, thy word is settled in heaven.* The Lord revealed His will to us through His Word. Look up the bible for your situations and everything promised therein for the Church belongs to you. You have the right to claim God's promises for your life and the authority to enforce God's will for your life against all opposition. We are fighting spiritual warfare through spiritual means, not carnal means. No weapon formed against you shall prosper. Obtain and use the power within to give God glory, achieve your purpose, and live an abundant life in this life and the life to come. Use the power!

Also Available from Apostolic Pentecostal Alliance Books LLC

www.apabooksllc.com

Bible Study Notes Version of Using Power Within

This 16 page 8.5" X 11" booklet is ideal for your bible study class with five lessons, lesson outline, and review focus questions.

Happiness as an Independent Variable Second Edition

Wouldn't you rather be happy instead of sad, angry, or worried? Our traditional perceptions and common understandings of happiness oftentimes fail to lead us to true happiness. With this book, you will discover that happiness must be treated as an independent variable if you are to have and maintain the long-term state of happiness. This is available in printed and e-book editions.

www.ingramcontent.com/pod-product-compliance
Lightning Source LLC
Chambersburg PA
CBHW052132010526
44113CB00034B/1893